Contents

People in the story

Emma Woodhouse

Mr Woodhouse

Miss Taylor / Mrs Weston

Isabella Woodhouse

Mr Weston

Mr Knightley

Mr John Knightley

Harriet Smith – Emma's friend

New words

ball

carriage

countryside

frame

strawberry

vicar

wedding

Note about the story

Jane Austen (1775–1817) wrote six novels which are still well-loved today. *Emma* (1815) and *Pride and Prejudice* (1813) (also in the Penguin Readers series at Level 4), are two of her most famous novels.

In *Emma*, Jane Austen writes about the **imaginary*** small town of Highbury, in the **countryside**, near London. There were no trains then, so the only way of travelling was on foot, by horse or by **carriage**. People have quiet lives in Highbury and enjoy walking, reading, art and music. Everyone knows their place in **society**, which comes from their family, how much money they have and how **educated** they are.

Emma Woodhouse is a very rich young woman, who lives with her father in their large house, Hartfield. At the time, most young women like Emma planned to get married. Few women had jobs, but some single (unmarried) women became governesses, living with a family and teaching their children. Emma does not need to marry, but she knows how important **marriage** is for other people and she loves **match-making**.

Before-reading questions

1 Read the back cover and look at the pictures in the book. What do you think the story will be about?

2 What do you know about women's lives at this time? Have you read any other stories written about this time? If yes, which ones?

*Definitions of words in **bold** can be found in the glossary on pages 78–80.

CHAPTER ONE

A wedding and a sad change

Emma Woodhouse was beautiful, clever and rich. She had a comfortable home and a happy **nature**, and for nearly twenty-one years had very little to **trouble** her.

She lived at Hartfield House with her loving father and her dear governess, Miss Taylor. Emma's older sister, Isabella, was married and lived in London, sixteen miles away. Their mother died when they were very young and Emma could not remember her. Miss Taylor was like a mother to the girls and later, as the years passed, was not just Emma's governess, but her dear friend. By the age of twenty, Emma always listened to Miss Taylor's **opinion**, and then did just what she wanted.

Then Emma felt her first **sadness**. Miss Taylor got married. Now she was Mrs Weston and Hartfield was no longer her home.

On the day of her dear friend's **wedding**, while her father slept after a quiet dinner, Emma sat thinking. Her friend was going only half a mile from them, to a house called Randalls, but having Mrs Weston half a mile away was very different from having Miss Taylor in the house.

"I know that I brought Miss Taylor and Mr Weston together myself, but now I'm going to lose my only friend," Emma thought. "Isabella won't visit until Christmas and now it's only October." Emma knew many people in the small town of Highbury, but she could not call one of them a friend. The Woodhouses were the most important family there and Emma had no **equal**.

Mr Woodhouse woke up from his sleep. He was an **anxious** man, who was easily worried and hated change.

"Poor Miss Taylor!" he cried. "It's very sad that she has gone."

"Papa, Mr Weston is an excellent man and we must be happy that he has found a good wife. His first wife died so long ago, and he has been alone since his son was **adopted**," Emma said. She wanted to help her father, so she was as **cheerful** as possible.

After the wedding, they were both very **pleased** to have a visit from a neighbour who was a close friend. Mr Knightley, an intelligent man of thirty-seven, was the older brother of Isabella's husband, Mr John Knightley.

"It's very kind of you to visit, Mr Knightley. It's so cold and wet – I hope you won't get ill," said Mr Woodhouse, anxiously.

"I'm happy to come, sir. It's a short walk from Donwell and it's a beautiful night," replied Mr Knightley. "I want to hear about the wedding. Did it go well? Who cried the most?"

"The wedding was **perfect** and no one cried," said Emma cheerfully. "Randalls is so close and we will meet the Westons every day."

"Dear Emma is very brave, but it is a great sadness for her to lose poor Miss Taylor," said Mr Woodhouse.

"Of course, but Emma knows that her friend now has a home of her own and a good husband to take care of her," said Mr Knightley.

"And I'm happy, too, because I made the **match** myself," said Emma, smiling.

"You just made a lucky guess," he said, shaking his head at her.

"It was more than luck," replied Emma. "I **encouraged** Mr Weston's visits here."

"Two intelligent people like Mr Weston and Miss Taylor can safely **manage** their own lives. **Match-making** is dangerous, Emma – I think you will hurt yourself more than help other people," said Mr Knightley.

"Dear Emma never thinks of herself if she can help others," said Mr Woodhouse, not really understanding. "But Emma, please don't make any more matches. They bring too much sad change to our family **circle**."

"Not for myself, Papa, but I must make matches for other people. I must look for a wife for Mr Elton, our poor **vicar**. He has been here for a year and should not be single any longer."

"Mr Elton is a handsome young man and I like him very much," replied Mr Woodhouse. "But if you want to be kind to him, my dear, ask him to dinner."

"I agree with you, sir," said Mr Knightley, laughing. "Invite Mr Elton to dinner, Emma, but allow him to choose his own wife."

———

During the quiet autumn days without Miss Taylor, Emma did her best to keep her father cheerful. Mr Woodhouse enjoyed **company**, but his circle of friends was very small. He did not often leave home, and hated both large parties and late nights.

Mr and Mrs Weston and Mr Knightley often came to Hartfield, and Mr Elton was now invited, too. A group of three ladies also visited often: Mrs Goddard, Mrs Bates and her single daughter, Miss Bates. They were brought in Mr Woodhouse's **carriage** to drink tea and play cards. Emma was happy for her father, but her evenings with these old ladies were long and **dull**.

One morning soon after, a letter came for Emma from

Mrs Goddard, who had a school for girls in Highbury. She wanted to bring one of her pupils to Hartfield, a pretty girl of seventeen called Harriet Smith. Emma was very happy to agree.

No one knew anything about Harriet's family. She was the '**natural**' daughter of a man rich enough to pay for her school, but no one knew who he was. She was very friendly with two young ladies from school, the Martin sisters, and stayed with them in the holidays. The Martin family rented one of Mr Knightley's farms, and Emma knew that he had a high opinion of them.

Harriet was small and very pretty. She was blonde, with blue eyes, and had a very sweet nature. "Her **manners** are as lovely as her face," Emma thought, when Harriet visited Hartfield. Harriet was happy that someone as important as Miss Woodhouse took an interest in her.

During Harriet's first visit, Emma decided that she could help her. "I can teach her," she thought, "and introduce her to **superior** people. Harriet isn't clever, but I need a new friend, now that Mrs Weston is married. There's nothing I can do for Mrs Weston now, but I can do everything for Harriet."

CHAPTER TWO
A new friend

Emma and Harriet quickly became friends, and Harriet was often at Hartfield with Emma's other visitors, Mr and Mrs Weston, Mr Knightley and Mr Elton. Harriet loved to tell Emma about her summer visit to the Martins, and often spoke of her friends' brother, Mr Robert Martin.

"He's very clever and everyone has a high opinion of him," Harriet told Emma. "His mother is sure that he'll be a very good husband for someone."

Emma was surprised and worried when she heard that Robert Martin was a single man. "What does he look like?" she asked Harriet.

"He's not very handsome. Well, I thought so at first, but now I'm not so sure," Harriet answered.

"Harriet, I'm sure he's a nice young man," replied Emma. "But if he marries, you should not be friends with his wife. I don't think she will be **educated** or your equal."

"I don't think Mr Martin will marry an **uneducated** girl," said Harriet. "But, if he does, I won't visit her."

After this conversation, Emma watched her new friend carefully. "She does speak about Mr Martin very often, but I'm sure she doesn't love him," Emma said to herself.

The next day, when Emma and Harriet were walking together on Donwell Road, they met Mr Martin. Emma waited while Harriet spoke to him.

"Well, Miss Woodhouse, is he as you **imagined**?" Harriet said excitedly, when he was gone.

"I agree that he's not handsome," said Emma, "but most of all, he's not a **gentleman**."

"Of course, he doesn't have Mr Knightley's excellent manners," said Harriet.

"But Mr Knightley is so fine that you cannot **compare** Mr Martin with him," replied Emma. "Compare Mr Martin with another gentleman – Mr Elton. I think he wants to **please** you."

"Mr Elton is the perfect husband for Harriet," Emma said to herself. "She will soon stop thinking about Robert Martin."

Mr Knightley was one of the few people who could see any **faults** in Emma. He was worried about Emma and Harriet becoming close friends.

"I'm afraid it may not be good for either of them," he said to Mrs Weston one day.

"Our opinions are very different," Mrs Weston replied. "I think it's good for Emma to have something new to do. Harriet isn't clever, but Emma can teach her."

"I believe someone like Harriet is the worst friend that Emma could have," said Mr Knightley. "She knows nothing herself, and thinks that Emma knows everything. And Harriet will soon start to feel uncomfortable with her place in **society**."

"Emma won't make any bad mistakes and I want her to be happy," said Mrs Weston. "Who knows what her future will be? She might never marry because poor Mr Woodhouse could not manage without her. Emma may have little faults, but where could you find a better daughter, or a kinder friend? And how well she looked last night! Can you imagine anyone more beautiful?"

"I agree with you," said Mr Knightley, smiling. "And I also want Emma to be happy."

Neither Mrs Weston nor Mr Knightley knew anything of Emma's plans for Harriet. But Emma was soon sure that Mr Elton was almost in love with Harriet already.

"Miss Smith was already beautiful, but in my opinion

you have added what she needed," Mr Elton told Emma one day.

"I'm happy that you think I've been useful to her, but she only needed a little help," said Emma. "Truly, I've never met anyone with such a lovely nature!"

The way that Mr Elton **sighed** told Emma that he was a man in love, and she was very happy. She was even more sure that he loved Harriet when she spoke to him a few days later.

"I've had an idea, Mr Elton. I would like to draw Harriet's picture."

"Yes, how wonderful! Please do it, Miss Woodhouse," replied Mr Elton. "I've seen your drawings here at Hartfield, and I think it's an excellent idea."

Harriet agreed and the picture was begun. While Emma worked, Mr Elton always stood behind her, watching everything and sighing. She was pleased that he stood where he could look at Harriet, but it was difficult to work with him there. He thought that her drawing of Harriet was perfect, which she thought was a little **foolish**.

When the picture was finished, Emma showed it to her father and friends.

"You've made her too tall, Emma," Mr Knightley told her. Emma knew that he was right. But Mr Elton could not find any fault with the picture.

"Oh no, she's not too tall!" said Mr Elton. "She's sitting down and it gives a perfect idea of Miss Smith."

"It's very pretty," said Mr Woodhouse. "I don't know

anybody who draws as beautifully as you. The only thing I don't like is that she seems to be sitting outside. It makes me worried that she'll catch a cold."

"But Papa, in my drawing it is summer," said Emma.

"But it's never safe to sit outside, my dear," said her father.

"Sir, to me it's just right to have Miss Smith outside," said Mr Elton. "Oh, I cannot keep my eyes from it! Miss Woodhouse, will you allow me to take it to London to buy a **frame** for it? It would make me very happy."

Emma could not **refuse**.

CHAPTER THREE
Two men in love

The day that Mr Elton went to London to get a frame for the picture, Harriet came hurrying to Hartfield.

"Please read this, Miss Woodhouse!" cried Harriet. She was holding a letter. "Mr Martin has asked me to marry him! He says that he loves me very much. I'm so surprised that I don't know what to do."

Emma read the letter. Mr Martin wrote well, almost like a gentleman.

"Is it a good letter?" asked Harriet, anxiously.

"It is," replied Emma, carefully. "It's so good that I believe one of his sisters helped him."

"But how shall I answer him? Dear Miss Woodhouse, do tell me."

"Oh, I cannot tell you what to say," replied Emma. "You will write your letter very well, I'm sure. You must tell him how sorry you are to hurt him . . . "

"You think I should refuse him then?" said Harriet.

"What do you mean, Harriet? I thought you were asking me *how* to write your answer." Harriet was silent. "Are you planning to say yes?" continued Emma in surprise.

"No . . . that is . . . Oh, please, Miss Woodhouse, tell me what I should do!"

"Harriet, I cannot. This is something you must decide for yourself."

"I had no idea that he liked me so much," said Harriet after a while.

"I cannot give you advice about **marriage**," said Emma. "But I believe that if a woman cannot decide, then she should say no."

"Yes, marriage is a very **serious** thing . . . " said Harriet. "I think it will be safer to say no."

Emma waited quietly. At last Harriet said, "I've decided what to do – to refuse Mr Martin. Do you think I'm right?"

"I do, dear Harriet!" cried Emma. "Now that you've decided, I cannot keep my **feelings** to myself. I could not visit Mr Martin's wife, so we could no longer be friends."

"I never thought of that," said Harriet. "I would like to be your friend always."

So Harriet's reply to Robert Martin was written, with Emma's help, and sent. Harriet was safe.

Harriet was quiet all evening. Emma waited before speaking of Mr Elton.

"Mr Martin will have my letter now. Do you think he's very unhappy, and his sisters, too?" sighed Harriet.

"Let's think of other friends, who may be happier," said Emma. "Maybe at this moment Mr Elton is showing your picture to his mother."

Harriet gave a small smile, and soon her smiles grew stronger.

The next time Mr Knightley visited Hartfield, he spoke to Emma alone about Harriet.

"I believe that your friend will soon have some good news. Robert Martin came to talk to me two evenings ago. He's very much in love with Harriet and would like to marry her."

"Well, I can tell you something, too," said Emma, smiling. "Mr Martin wrote to Harriet yesterday and she refused him."

"Then she's more foolish than I thought!" said Mr Knightley, crossly. "Did you encourage her to say no?"

"I will not answer that, but I will say this – Mr Martin may be an excellent young man, but he's not Harriet's equal," said Emma.

"Why do you think her superior to Robert Martin?" said Mr Knightley, loudly. "She's someone's natural daughter, with no money and no family. She's pretty and has a nice nature, and that is all."

"Harriet should not pay for the mistakes of her parents. She does not know who her father is, but he could be a gentleman. She was educated with gentlemen's daughters and should not be a farmer's wife," answered Emma.

"Until you made her your friend, Harriet was happy with her place," said Mr Knightley. "She was happy with the Martins in the summer. You have not been a good friend to Harriet Smith, Emma. If she marries Robert Martin, she will be safe and happy with a man who loves her. If you teach her to want more, she may stay single forever."

"We should stop talking about it, Mr Knightley, because it will only make us both more angry. Harriet has already refused Robert Martin."

Emma did not like **quarrelling** with Mr Knightley and very much wanted him to leave. He sat opposite her, looking angry, and some minutes passed before he spoke again.

"You do not hide your love of match-making," he said at last, "and I must tell you something, as your friend. If you think Elton is the man for Harriet, you're making a mistake. He will not marry someone who is below him in society."

Then Mr Knightley got up, said good morning, and walked off quickly.

After this **quarrel**, it was some time before Mr Knightley came to Hartfield again. When he did, he looked serious and Emma knew that he was still angry with her. But Emma could not be sorry about Harriet refusing Robert Martin.

She was sure that Mr Elton was in love with her friend.

Mr Elton came back cheerfully from London with the picture of Harriet, which was put on the wall in the little sitting room. He looked at it often, and sighed like a man in love.

"Oh, Harriet," said Emma, "I'm sure he will soon ask you to marry him."

"Dear Miss Woodhouse!" said Harriet. "I must believe it because you're always right. But Mr Elton is so superior! Can he really want to marry me?"

"Dear Harriet, I believe it's a perfect match. Now we just need to wait."

It was almost Christmas and the day of Isabella's visit to Hartfield arrived. Mr Woodhouse was very anxious about the long journey that she and her family had to make by carriage from London. But Isabella and John Knightley, and their five children, managed the sixteen miles **perfectly** happily. The house was immediately filled with noise, which Mr Woodhouse could **bear** for a short time because it was his dear family. The children were soon sent away to play and eat and sleep, while the adults talked together quietly.

The next day, Mr Knightley came. Emma was playing with Isabella's new baby when he walked into the sitting room. She hoped they could be friends again, after their quarrel. He sat with Emma and took the baby on his knee, laughing.

"Our opinions about men and women are very different," said Emma, "but I'm happy that we feel the same way about our nephews and nieces."

"Oh, Emma, if you stop imagining what is best for other people, we might always agree," he answered.

"Are you saying that our quarrels are always because I'm wrong?" said Emma with a smile.

"Yes, because I'm sixteen years older than you!" said Mr Knightley, laughing. "Now let's be friends and say no more about it." Emma happily agreed.

CHAPTER FOUR
A Christmas party

Mr and Mrs Weston invited the Woodhouse and Knightley families to a dinner party at Randalls on Christmas Eve. Harriet and Mr Elton were invited, too. But the day before the party, Harriet caught a cold and was too ill to go.

"Mr Elton won't come now, if Harriet cannot be there," Emma said to herself. So she was very surprised when she heard Mr Elton speaking about it to her brother-in-law, Mr John Knightley. Then she heard him agreeing to go in John Knightley's carriage.

"Well," said Emma to herself. "It's strange that he still wants to go to the party, when Harriet cannot go."

Isabella and her father went to Randalls together in Mr Woodhouse's carriage, while Mr John Knightley and Emma went to get Mr Elton. It was very cold and a little snow began to fall as the carriages left Hartfield.

"I never saw a man want to please the ladies as much as Mr Elton," said Mr John Knightley, as he and Emma travelled to Mr Elton's house. "And to please you, most of all."

"Me! Are you imagining Mr Elton to be in love with me? What an idea!" said Emma.

"I'm only asking you if he might be. I think you **encourage** him."

"No, no. Mr Elton and I are only good friends," Emma replied. She did not like her brother-in-law giving her advice and said no more.

"People often make foolish mistakes when they don't understand something," she said to herself.

When Mr Elton got into their carriage, Emma talked to him about Harriet, but he soon moved on to other things. "It's strange that he has forgotten Harriet already," she thought.

When they arrived at Randalls, Emma often found Mr Elton at her side, asking her questions. Was she warm enough? Was her father comfortable? She could hear Mr Weston speaking about his son, and she wanted to listen. But she had to be **polite** to Mr Elton.

Frank Churchill was Mr Weston's son from his first marriage and he was just a baby when his mother died. He was adopted by his rich uncle and aunt, Mr and Mrs Churchill, who were Mr Weston's brother and sister-in-law. Mr Weston saw his son every year in London, but Frank never came to Highbury.

Emma found Frank Churchill very interesting. They were the same age and their families were close friends. "I don't plan to marry," Emma sometimes said to herself. "But if I ever do, he could be the perfect husband." Mr and Mrs Weston never spoke of it, but Emma was sure they felt the same.

At dinner, Emma was pleased to be sitting next to Mr Weston, who soon told her his news about Frank.

"I had a letter from Frank this morning – he'll be here in two weeks. He has wanted to come since September, but he always has to do what his aunt wants," Mr Weston said.

"I'm very happy that she has allowed him to visit you at last," said Emma.

After dinner, the ladies went to the sitting room and Emma sat with Mrs Weston, talking about Frank's visit.

"I'm worried that he won't come this time, either," Mrs Weston told her. "I think Mrs Churchill will decide again that she cannot manage without him."

At that moment, Mr Elton came into the sitting room, and sat down on the sofa between Emma and Mrs Weston. Emma was pleased that he talked about Harriet, but suddenly he seemed more anxious about Emma catching Harriet's cold than about Harriet.

"Promise me that you won't visit Harriet again until she's better!" he cried.

Emma was cross. John Knightley could not be right, could he? She gave Mr Elton a cold look, which she hoped he could understand, and went to sit with her sister.

Suddenly, Mr John Knightley hurried into the room with the news that it was snowing heavily. For a while everyone talked about what they should do. Would the roads be safe? Should they stay at Randalls for the night?

Then Mr Knightley went outside and came back into the room. "The snow isn't thick yet," he said. "There will be no problem travelling home, if the carriages leave now."

Mr Woodhouse hurried to his carriage, followed by Isabella. Mr John Knightley climbed in quickly behind his wife, forgetting that he should travel in the other carriage. Emma had to travel alone with Mr Elton.

As soon as the carriage was out of the drive, Mr Elton reached for her hand and began to speak quickly.

"Miss Woodhouse, you must know how I feel about you! I'm ready to die if you refuse me!" he cried.

Emma was **shocked**. Was the man who loved Harriet asking her to marry him? How could this be happening?

"Mr Elton, I'm very surprised that you say these things to me, and not my friend, Miss Smith," Emma said.

"Why do you speak of Miss Smith? I only care about her as your friend!" cried Mr Elton. "Who can think of Miss Smith when Miss Woodhouse is near?"

Emma was too shocked to reply. She pulled her hand away, but Mr Elton tried to take it again and said, "Lovely Miss Woodhouse, I believe that you have understood me."

"No, sir!" cried Emma. "I have always believed that you loved Miss Smith."

"Miss Smith? Never! She is not my equal. My visits to Hartfield have been only for you, and you gave me hope."

"Mr Elton, I did not encourage you," said Emma, coldly. "Please do not speak to me of marriage."

Mr Elton was too angry to say any more. The carriage was going very slowly because of the snow, and it was a few more minutes before they reached Mr Elton's house. He jumped out of the carriage without another word.

At home, Emma first had to look after her father. Then, alone in her room, she could sit down and think. What a terrible mistake! And poor Harriet! That was the worst thing of all.

She thought back over the last few weeks. "I was sure that the picture showed Mr Elton's feelings for Harriet," she said to herself. "Mr Elton is the opposite of what I imagined. He cares little about the feelings of other people. He didn't speak to me like a man in love. He only wants a rich wife. If he cannot have Miss Woodhouse of

Hartfield with thirty thousand pounds, he'll soon want to marry Miss Somebody with twenty, or ten thousand." Then she remembered what Mr Knightley said. "He could see Mr Elton's true nature then, and I can only see it now," thought Emma.

She could not feel sorry for Mr Elton, but she was very sorry for Harriet. It was foolish to try to bring two people together. "Harriet only thought about Mr Elton because of me. I was right to stop her marrying Mr Martin, but that was all."

Emma felt a little more cheerful the next morning, and the weather helped her. Thick snow lay on the ground, and for four days she could not go out. She could not see Harriet, and she did not need to explain to her father why Mr Elton did not visit them. But Emma could not be happy, knowing that she still had to give the painful news to Harriet.

A few days later, the snow was gone and Isabella and her family went back to London. The same day, a letter arrived for Mr Woodhouse from Mr Elton. "He's leaving Highbury tomorrow, to visit friends in Bath," Mr Woodhouse told Emma, sadly. But to Emma this was very good news. She now had to tell Harriet the truth.

When she was told, Harriet cried for a long time, but she was not angry with anyone. Emma was as kind as possible. She invited Harriet to Hartfield often, and did everything she could to stop Harriet thinking of Mr Elton.

CHAPTER FIVE
A visitor to Highbury

Like most people in Highbury, Emma was very excited about their new visitor. But Mrs Weston was right and Frank Churchill did not come.

"Mr and Mrs Weston are very **disappointed**. Frank's aunt will not allow him to leave her," Emma told Mr Knightley one day.

"Frank Churchill should visit his father, and meet his father's new wife. He has both money and time. I heard he was in Weymouth a little while ago. So it is possible for him to leave Mrs Churchill. A man can always do the right thing, if he chooses to do it," said Mr Knightley.

"You have decided to think badly of him without knowing him," said Emma.

"I would be happy to hear good things about Frank Churchill," said Mr Knightley. "But I have only heard that he's handsome and has nice manners."

"A handsome young man with nice manners is enough for me," said Emma, laughing. "And everyone in Highbury agrees with me – they speak of Frank Churchill all the time."

"Well, I don't think of him from one month to the next," said Mr Knightley, crossly.

Emma began to talk about something different. She did not want to quarrel with Mr Knightley again.

"Why was he so cross about a young man that he hasn't even met?" she said to herself later.

But Emma knew that Mr Knightley was right about some things. She knew, for example, that she should be kinder to Mrs and Miss Bates, the old ladies who were her father's friends. They had very little money because Mrs Bates's husband died long ago, and Miss Bates never married. Mr Knightley often spoke of them and encouraged Emma to visit them. But they were so dull! Miss Bates was a kind and cheerful woman, but she talked a lot about uninteresting things. And most of all, she talked about her niece, Jane Fairfax, or read Jane's letters aloud to visitors. Emma and Jane were the same age and everyone thought they should be good friends. Emma tried to like Jane, but she could not. She thought that Jane was cold and unfriendly. Miss Bates thought that her niece was perfect, and worried about her all the time, which Emma found very **annoying**.

Emma knew that she should feel sorry for Jane, who was the only child of Mrs Bates's youngest daughter. Her parents died when she was a small child, so she was looked after by her grandmother and her aunt. But some rich friends of her father's, Mr and Mrs Campbell, wanted to **adopt** the little girl and educate her. When Jane was nine, she went to live with the Campbells and became like a sister to their only daughter. Mr Campbell wanted Jane to become a governess. With a job, she could look after herself even if she could not find a husband.

Jane was now twenty-one, and her friend, Miss Campbell,

was married. Emma knew that Jane had to get a job as a governess soon.

One morning, Emma was walking with Harriet in Highbury, when they came near Mrs and Miss Bates's house. Harriet was sighing over Mr Elton and Emma wanted her to stop.

"Let's visit Mrs and Miss Bates," Emma said to her friend. "They will not have another letter from Jane Fairfax yet, so it will be safe to visit."

Miss Bates was very pleased to see them. She gave them the best seats, brought out a cake, and talked without stopping. Emma tried to listen **politely**. Then Miss Bates said, "We've had the most surprising news, Miss Woodhouse. This morning we had a letter from our dear Jane! I've read it twice to Mother already."

Emma was thinking that she and Harriet might be able to escape before the letter was read to them, too.

But Miss Bates talked on. "We haven't seen Jane for two years, but now we will see her again! She arrives next week. She will be here for three months, or even longer, because Mr and Mrs Campbell are going to Ireland to visit their daughter. You know that their daughter is married and living in Ireland now with her new husband? Jane says Mr Dixon is such a handsome, **charming** man! Jane always wanted to go to Ireland before – Mr Dixon says it is so beautiful. And we all think so well of Mr Dixon – we remember Jane's terrible accident in Weymouth. He stopped our dear Jane from falling into the sea!"

Emma had an idea about Jane Fairfax and this handsome young man. "I can guess why Jane does not want to go to Ireland, now that this charming young man is the husband of her best friend," she thought. "She might be in love with the man who saved her life!"

"That is surprising news," Emma replied, politely. "So Jane is coming here, not going to Ireland to see her dear friend, Mrs Dixon?"

"Yes, that's what Jane prefers. She hasn't been well and she will get better here. But I can read her letter to you and you will hear everything!"

"I'm so sorry, Miss Bates, but we really cannot stay any longer. My father will be anxious." And Emma and Harriet happily escaped without having to hear Jane's letter.

After this, Emma decided that she must try to like Jane

Fairfax more. "She has no money of her own and has to get a job as a governess," Emma said to herself. "And I'm sure that she's in love with Mr Dixon and is coming to Highbury to be away from him."

When Jane arrived in Highbury, Emma invited her and her aunt to Hartfield. But after an afternoon in their company, Emma felt the same as before about both of them. Miss Bates talked all the time, and Jane said almost nothing. Emma asked her about Weymouth and the Dixons, but Jane said very little. She said nothing about Frank Churchill either, who was in Weymouth at the same time.

"We were very disappointed that Mr Churchill could not come to Highbury," Emma told her. "We are very excited to meet him. Is he very handsome?"

"People seem to think so," was Jane's only answer.

Then Miss Bates had some surprising news. "Have you heard that Mr Elton is getting married, Miss Woodhouse?"

Emma was shocked. "I hope he will be very happy," she managed to say.

"Yes, he has met a young lady in Bath and they will come to Highbury after the wedding. So we will have a new neighbour. Isn't it wonderful news?"

When her visitors were gone, Emma could think quietly about the news alone. She was very happy about it for herself, but very sorry for Harriet. She should tell her as soon as possible. But at that very moment, Harriet came to visit her.

"I've just met Robert Martin with his sister in a shop," Harriet cried. "He was so friendly towards me, Miss Woodhouse. It was so nice to see him again!"

Then Emma gave her the news about Mr Elton, and the next moment Harriet began to cry about Mr Elton once more.

"Robert Martin is a better man than Mr Elton," Emma said to herself. "But he's only a farmer, so Harriet must forget about him, and about Mr Elton, too!"

The next day, Mr Martin and Mr Elton were both forgotten when Mrs Weston hurried to Hartfield with a letter from Frank Churchill.

"He's coming tomorrow at four o'clock!" Mrs Weston cried. "Think of me then, dear Emma!"

CHAPTER SIX
Another new visitor

At twelve o'clock the next day, Emma was in her room, thinking about Frank Churchill. She imagined Mrs Weston at Randalls, checking his bedroom to see that everything was perfect.

As Emma walked down the stairs, she heard voices in the sitting room. She opened the door and was very surprised to find Mr Weston and a young gentleman with her father. The two visitors stood up as she entered the room.

"Emma, may I introduce my son, Frank Churchill?" Mr Weston said, smiling happily.

The interesting young man that everyone spoke about so often was actually in front of her. He was a very good-looking young man, with perfect manners.

"I arrived home a day early," Frank explained.

Frank Churchill was a very charming and friendly young man. He talked to Emma about how lovely Randalls was, and Hartfield, too. He wanted to know what people did in Highbury. Did they enjoy music and dancing? Emma noticed how pleased Mr Weston looked to see Frank and her talking so happily together.

After a while, Mr Weston got up to go. "I have things to do in town, but you don't need to hurry away, Frank," he said.

But Frank stood up, too. "Well, there are some

people I should visit – a lady called Miss Fairfax, who is staying with Mrs and Miss Bates. Do you know them?"

"Yes, we know them well! You met Miss Fairfax in Weymouth, I believe?" replied Mr Weston.

"Yes, but it's not important. I can go another day," said Frank.

"You must visit Miss Fairfax today," said his father. "You must be polite to her."

"You're right," Frank replied, and left Emma with the promise to visit Hartfield again soon.

Frank Churchill came again the next morning, this time with Mrs Weston. He asked Emma to walk with them through Highbury. He was very interested in everything. He wanted to see the church, and the shops, and the house where his father lived before Randalls. When the three of them got to The Crown Hotel, he stopped to look inside the building. He noticed the large **ballroom**, which was no longer used.

"But there should be a **ball** here every week! It's not possible to do without dancing!" he said. Emma laughed and they left The Crown to continue their walk. As they passed the Bates's house, Emma remembered his visit there the day before.

"Did you see Miss Fairfax often at Weymouth?" asked Emma.

"Yes, I did. I know the Campbells well and I like them very much," said Frank.

"Did you know that Miss Fairfax is going to leave them soon, to be a governess?"

"Yes," he answered quietly. Then he said, "Did you ever hear her play the piano?"

"Of course," replied Emma. "Remember that I've known her since we were children. She plays beautifully."

"I thought so, but I wanted the opinion of someone who knows about music. In Weymouth, Mr Dixon always asked Miss Fairfax to play, not Miss Campbell – before they were married, I mean."

"That sounds difficult for both Miss Fairfax and Miss Campbell," said Emma.

"Well, they all seemed happy, but you know Miss Fairfax better than I do," said Frank.

37

"I've known her a long time, but she's always so quiet," said Emma. "Miss Fairfax and I have very different natures, which makes it difficult for us to be close friends."

Frank agreed with her. "He's so easy to talk to," Emma thought.

But Emma's good opinion of Frank Churchill was a little shaken the next day. She heard he was in London, getting his hair cut. "How strange to travel sixteen miles and back for a haircut!" she said to herself.

When Mr Knightley heard about it, he said, "Hmm, he's just the foolish young man I thought he was." Emma did not reply.

Frank came back from London with his hair cut. He laughed at himself, and Emma laughed with him. She began to think that Frank Churchill was good enough, or at least nearly good enough, to be in love with her.

A few days later, Emma was invited to a large dinner party given by some neighbours, Mr and Mrs Cole. Frank Churchill, Mr and Mrs Weston and Mr Knightley were invited, too. Harriet, Jane Fairfax and some other young ladies were invited to join them after dinner.

At dinner, Emma was very happy to be sitting next to Frank. Soon everyone began to talk about Jane Fairfax.

"When I visited Miss Bates today there was a beautiful piano in the house," said Mrs Cole. "It arrived yesterday from London and Miss Fairfax has no idea who sent it. She thought it might be a gift from Mr Campbell, but he didn't say anything about it in his last letter to her."

"Why are you smiling?" Emma asked Frank quietly.

"Why are you?" he answered.

"Because why would Mr Campbell keep it a secret? I don't think it was from him," said Emma. "Maybe it was from Mrs Dixon?"

"Ah, I didn't think of her," said Frank. "Yes, I agree. It's a present from Mr and Mrs Dixon. We were speaking the other day about how Mr Dixon preferred Miss Fairfax's playing."

"Yes, and I'm sure that he loves more than her music," said Emma quietly. "I cannot help thinking that there is something between Mr Dixon and Miss Fairfax. Why did she come to Highbury and not go to Ireland? And he saved her life, you know. I'm sure we'll soon hear that the piano is a present from Mr and Mrs Dixon. But Miss Fairfax will know that it's really from Mr Dixon."

"Yes, I think you're right and it's a gift of love," agreed Frank.

After dinner, Harriet, Jane Fairfax and Miss Bates arrived, together with some other young ladies, and the party moved to the sitting room. Everyone wanted to talk to Jane about the piano. Emma saw that Jane **blushed** when she spoke about it. Frank said good evening to Miss Bates and Jane, and sat down opposite them, next to Emma again.

Emma knew that everyone must notice them together. Frank talked happily about Enscombe, in Yorkshire, where he lived with the Churchills. He told her how much he loved Highbury and enjoyed the company of everyone there. Then Mr Cole came over and Emma turned away from Frank for a moment to speak to him. When she turned back, Frank was looking at Jane Fairfax.

"What's the matter?" asked Emma.

"Oh, I'm sorry," answered Frank. "But look, Miss Fairfax has done her hair in such a strange way. Shall I go and ask her if that's the way they do it in Ireland? You can see if she blushes. Yes, I will!" He got up immediately and went to speak to Jane Fairfax. But he was standing in front of her, so Emma could not see her face. Mrs Weston then came and sat in Frank's chair.

"What a wonderful party!" she said. "Did you know that Miss Bates and Miss Fairfax came in Mr Knightley's carriage and will go home in it? What a kind thing for him to think of!"

"Mr Knightley is always ready to do something useful for other people. And he does it quietly, without wanting people to notice," said Emma.

"An idea has come into my head," said Mrs Weston. "What do you say to a match between Mr Knightley and Jane Fairfax?"

"Mr Knightley and Jane Fairfax!" cried Emma. "No, it's impossible! How could you think that?"

"But you know that Miss Fairfax has always been a favourite of his," said Mrs Weston.

"No, you're quite wrong," said Emma. "His good nature explains everything. He's always very kind to Mrs and

Miss Bates, even when Jane Fairfax isn't with them. Dear Mrs Weston, don't begin match-making. You do it very badly! Mr Knightley doesn't want to marry. He's happy by himself, with his farm and his sheep and his library, and he loves his brother's children. He doesn't need a wife."

"But Emma, I've had an idea about the piano. Everyone thinks that it's from the Campbells, but could it be from Mr Knightley?"

Emma did not like Mrs Weston's idea and she began to watch Mr Knightley carefully. When Jane was asked to play the piano, Emma noticed Mr Knightley watching her with interest.

"I hope Mrs Weston isn't right," Emma said to herself. "If Mr Knightley marries it will be bad for everyone – for John and Isabella, and their children, for Papa, and for me. I cannot bear the idea of a Mrs Knightley!"

Then Mr Knightley came to sit down next to her and spoke warmly about Jane's playing.

"Wasn't it kind of the Campbells to give Miss Fairfax the piano?" Emma said to him.

"Yes," he agreed, "but I do think surprises are foolish things."

"I don't think he sent Jane Fairfax the piano," Emma said to herself. "Mr Knightley does nothing secretly."

CHAPTER SEVEN
A new neighbour arrives

The next day, Emma was in Highbury when Miss Bates crossed the street towards her.

"Mr Churchill has come to hear Jane's new piano," she said. "Please come too, Miss Woodhouse, and tell us your opinion of it. I saw you from the window, you see." Emma went with Miss Bates, who did not stop talking all the way to her house.

"How lovely that you came!" said Frank, when they arrived.

Jane seemed anxious as she sat down at the piano. "Maybe she's thinking about Mr Dixon," Emma thought.

"What a wonderful piano!" said Frank, loudly. "Mr Campbell and all his friends in Ireland chose it very well." Jane did not look round.

"Stop it!" said Emma quietly, trying not to smile. "You must not **upset** her."

But Frank went on in a loud voice to Jane, "They sent music too, I see. How very kind of them. It shows how much they love you."

Emma saw a little smile on Jane's face. "Perfect. Jane Fairfax is enjoying her secret thoughts of Mr Dixon!" she said to herself.

"I think she understands you," she said to Frank.

"I hope she does," he answered. "I want her to understand me. You know, she's playing *his* favourite music at the moment. I remember that we danced to this music in Weymouth. Now, Miss Woodhouse, when will we have dancing in Highbury? We must plan a ball at The Crown Hotel ballroom, and you must promise me the first two dances."

———

Everyone agreed that the ball was an excellent idea. Jane Fairfax was unusually excited about it, and only Mr Knightley was not interested in it. But Emma had no time to quarrel with Mr Knightley about it because suddenly there was no ball. Frank had a letter from Mrs Churchill, asking him to go back to Yorkshire immediately because she was ill. Emma was very disappointed.

Frank came to Hartfield to say goodbye, and seemed very sad.

"I hope I will come back soon, if my aunt allows me," he said, "then we can still have our ball. And you must not forget your promise to dance with me."

"Are you leaving without saying goodbye to Highbury? You should visit Miss Bates – she would make you more cheerful!" Emma said with a smile.

"I did go there, just for five minutes. But only Miss Fairfax was at home and I had to wait for Miss Bates to come back . . . " Frank walked to the window. Then he turned round and looked at Emma. He seemed troubled. "Miss Woodhouse, I think you must already know the truth . . . "

Emma could guess what he wanted to say. "But I don't want him to tell me that he's in love with me yet," she thought.

"I think you were right to visit Miss Bates," she told Frank cheerfully, without looking at him.

He was silent and then she heard him sigh. "And now I have to say goodbye to Hartfield, where I've been so happy." He stopped again.

"He's very much in love with me," thought Emma. And then they were saying goodbye, and he was gone.

Emma felt very sorry. "We had fun together, and he almost told me that he loved me," she said to herself. "Now everything feels dull without him. I think I might be a little in love with him, too."

But the next day, she was cheerful again. "He's a nice young man, but he does have faults," she thought. And when she imagined him asking her to marry him, she always refused him.

After a few days, Emma had a letter from Frank. In it, he wrote of her beautiful little friend, Harriet, and Emma had an idea. "Harriet has such a warm and lovely nature. If Frank can stop loving me, Harriet might make him happy," she thought. "But no, I must not think about it. I know that match-making is dangerous."

————

While Frank was in Highbury, no one thought about Mr Elton. But Mr Elton was back in Highbury with his new wife and everyone was talking about him again. He seemed very pleased with himself for introducing a superior woman like his wife to Highbury.

Mrs Elton was invited to Hartfield and Emma did not like her at all. She talked a lot, but only about herself and her rich sister-in-law, who lived at Maple Grove, near Bath.

"Oh Miss Woodhouse, your beautiful house is so like Maple Grove," she said as she arrived. "And the gardens, too. My sister-in-law would love them. She is always pleased to see large gardens like hers."

Emma was sure that people with large gardens cared very little about other people's large gardens, but she said nothing.

"My sister-in-law and her husband will visit in the summer in their new carriage," Mrs Elton continued.

"They love visiting the **countryside**. I imagine you have many summer parties in the countryside, Miss Woodhouse?"

"No, we are very quiet people, who prefer to stay at home," replied Emma.

"Oh, no one can love staying at home more than me!" cried Mrs Elton. "We have already met many excellent people here," Mrs Elton went on. "I like both the Westons very much. I was surprised that Mrs Weston has such good manners. She was your governess, I believe?" Emma was too shocked to speak. "And who do you think came in while we were there? Knightley! Knightley himself. Mr E has spoken about his good friend so often, I was very pleased to meet him. Knightley is a gentleman. I like him very much."

Happily it was soon time for Mrs Elton to go.

"Terrible woman! She is worse than I thought!" Emma said to herself. "She imagines herself to be so important. She was shocked that my governess has good manners! She has never met Mr Knightley before and she called him Knightley! And she tells me that he's a gentleman!"

Emma's first opinion of Mrs Elton did not change. But Mrs Elton changed – she became cold and unfriendly towards Emma, and to Harriet, too. But Mrs Elton liked Jane Fairfax very much.

"I'm crazy about Jane Fairfax!" Emma heard her say. "What a sweet, interesting young woman! She's so clever and she plays the piano beautifully. I know enough about music to be sure of that. Oh, but poor thing – it's terrible that she has to become a governess. I will look out for a good job for her. I know so many people, I'm sure that I can help her."

Another time Emma heard Mrs Elton saying to Jane, "I hear you went to the post office in the rain! You could catch a cold. I won't allow you to do it again. The man who gets our letters from the post office can get yours too and bring them to you."

"No, you're very kind, but I cannot give up my walk," replied Jane.

Emma noticed how much Jane wanted to get her own letters. "She doesn't want anyone to see them," she thought. "I'm sure they are from Mr Dixon in Ireland."

CHAPTER EIGHT
Harriet is saved

Spring arrived, and with it some very good news from Randalls. Mr Weston came to Hartfield with a letter from Frank. Mrs Churchill was better and wanted to come down from Yorkshire to Richmond, which was only nine miles from Highbury.

"Frank will be able to visit Highbury often now. He will be with us very soon!" said Mr Weston.

When she heard the news, Emma felt sure that she was not in love. "I'll be pleased to see Frank Churchill, but only as a friend," she thought. "But will he still be in love with me?"

She did not have to wait long before Frank was back at Hartfield. She watched him carefully. He was friendly and seemed pleased to see her, but she did not think he was in love with her any more. But there was something troubling him and he did not stay long. He had another visit to make. "Maybe he's afraid he will fall in love with me again," Emma thought.

With Frank back in Highbury often, plans were quickly made for the ball at The Crown.

At the ball, Emma remembered her promise to dance with Frank first. While they were dancing, she noticed Mr Knightley standing at the side with the husbands and fathers. "He should dance," thought Emma. "He looks so young and handsome. Frank is the only man in the room who could be compared with him."

Everyone was enjoying themselves, but then Emma noticed Harriet. She was the only young lady who had no one to dance with. Mr Elton was standing near Harriet, speaking to Mrs Weston.

"Aren't you dancing, Mr Elton?" Mrs Weston asked him.

"Of course, Mrs Weston, if you will dance with me," he replied.

"Oh, I'm not dancing tonight. But I'm sure there is a young lady who would like to dance," said Mrs Weston, looking at Harriet.

"Miss Smith? Oh no, Mrs Weston, I'm an old married man now! My dancing days are finished."

Harriet heard it all and looked very **upset**. Emma was very angry. Then she saw Mr Elton walking over to talk to Mr Knightley. A minute later, she saw Mr Knightley dancing with Harriet. Emma felt wonderfully happy. Mr Elton walked away, looking very foolish.

Between the dances, Emma was able to thank Mr Knightley.

"Mr Elton was very unkind," said Mr Knightley.

"I was completely wrong about him," replied Emma. "I was sure he was in love with Harriet."

"I think you chose a better wife for him than he has chosen for himself. Harriet has a much nicer nature than Mrs Elton," said Mr Knightley.

At that moment, the music started again.

"Who are you going to dance with?" asked Mr Knightley.

"With you, if you will ask me," she replied.

"Will you dance, Emma?" he said, giving her his hand.

"Yes, I will," she said happily.

The next morning, Emma was walking in the garden, thinking about the ball, when Frank Churchill came up the drive with Harriet. Harriet was holding on to his arm, looking very white and frightened. Emma took them quickly into the house, and Harriet fell down on to a chair.

"What has happened?" Emma asked Frank, anxiously.

"She was walking with another young lady from

Mrs Goddard's, when they were stopped by some young boys who wanted money," Frank explained. "Her friend screamed and ran away, and soon there was a crowd of boys around Harriet, shouting at her. That's when I found her. The boys ran off when they saw me, and I brought Harriet here."

Frank stayed until he could see that Harriet was better, and then had to hurry away.

"How wonderful that Harriet was saved by Frank," thought Emma, later. "But of course I won't do anything to bring them together. I'll wait for things to happen by themselves."

A few days later, Harriet said to Emma, "I cannot believe I was ever in love with Mr Elton. I can see nothing nice in him now. I've fallen in love with someone very superior to me, and to everyone. I will never marry now."

"I'm not surprised, Harriet. He did a very good thing for you," said Emma.

"Oh, it was wonderful how he saved me! One moment I was so unhappy. Then the next moment I saw him coming, and I was perfectly happy!" cried Harriet.

"I'll never give you advice again," said Emma. "I'll only say this – it's true that he is your superior, but sometimes surprising matches are made. Wonderful things sometimes do happen."

———

The weather got warmer and Mrs Elton did not forget about her love of parties in the countryside. She made plans for a large picnic at Box Hill, which was in a lovely part of the countryside, seven miles from Highbury. But a few days before her picnic, one of her horses hurt its leg.

"Oh, Knightley, I am terribly disappointed," Mrs Elton told him. "At Maple Grove we always visited beautiful places at this time of year. What are we going to do?"

"Come to Donwell then, and pick the **strawberries**. You can do that without horses," said Mr Knightley.

"Oh, I would love to come!" said Mrs Elton. "I will tell everyone."

"No, Mrs Elton, please allow me to invite people to my own house," said Mr Knightley.

Emma was very pleased about the visit to Donwell. The Westons, Harriet and Jane Fairfax were invited, and Frank Churchill, too. And Mrs Elton's picnic at Box Hill was planned for the day after the visit to Donwell because the horse's leg got better so fast.

Two summer parties

It was a hot day in June when Emma and her friends walked across the fields to Donwell, while Mr Woodhouse was safely driven there in his carriage.

At Donwell, Mr Woodhouse went into the house, while the others stayed in the gardens. Mrs Elton, who was wearing a very large hat, talked loudly about the strawberries at Maple Grove.

"When is Frank arriving?" Emma asked Mr Weston.

"He is riding from Richmond," explained Mr Weston. "I hope nothing has happened to his horse. Mrs Weston will be very anxious if he doesn't arrive soon."

Then Mrs Elton was too hot and wanted to sit under the trees. Emma heard her talking excitedly to Jane about a job as a governess with a family she knew.

"They are a very superior family. You must allow me to write to them tomorrow," Mrs Elton was saying.

"I'm not ready to look for a job yet," Jane replied politely, but Mrs Elton would not listen and went on talking.

"Mr Knightley, will you show us around the gardens?" asked Jane, suddenly standing up.

Mr Knightley agreed and everyone walked around the beautiful park together. They came to a place which looked across the countryside, towards Mill Farm, where Robert

Martin lived. Then Emma noticed Mr Knightley talking to Harriet alone. "I'm pleased he's being kind to her," thought Emma.

The sun was very hot and everyone was happy when it was time to go into the house for lunch.

"Frank is very late," Mrs Weston said to her husband, anxiously. "Do you think he has fallen from his horse? Or that his aunt has stopped him coming?" Emma looked at Harriet, but Harriet did not look worried.

After lunch, Emma stayed in the house with her father. While he was sleeping, Emma walked into the hall, and Jane suddenly appeared from the garden, looking upset.

"Please would you tell the others that I've gone home?" she asked Emma. "It's late and I must get home to my aunt."

"Of course," replied Emma. "I will ask for the carriage for you."

Jane looked very unhappy. "No, thank you. You're very kind, Miss Woodhouse, but I prefer to walk. I need very much to be alone!"

Emma felt very sorry for her. "Mrs Elton was very annoying to Jane Fairfax today, and now she has to go home to her aunt," she thought.

Fifteen minutes later, Frank arrived looking very cross.

"My aunt felt unwell and I couldn't leave Richmond until very late. But it was stupid to come. It's much too hot and I hate hot weather!" he said. "I'll go back to Richmond as soon as I feel better because you're all going to leave soon.

I passed Miss Fairfax going home already. It's madness to walk in this weather!"

"I'm pleased I'm not in love with him," Emma said to herself, seeing Frank like this. "I wouldn't like a husband who gets so cross just because of hot weather. But Harriet has a sweet nature and it won't trouble her."

The sun was hot again the next day as the carriages drove to Box Hill. It was the same party of friends as the day before, but Miss Bates came with her niece and Mrs Weston stayed at home with Mr Woodhouse.

But at Box Hill no one seemed happy. The weather was too hot and everyone was quiet. The Eltons walked alone together, Mr Knightley stayed with Miss Bates and Jane, while Emma and Harriet were with Frank.

Emma was very bored. Frank was so silent and dull. But when they all sat down together for the picnic, Frank became more cheerful. He seemed to want to please her, and to make her laugh. She began to enjoy herself. She did not care if the others saw her **flirting** with Frank. She knew she could never be in love with him, and she wanted him to marry Harriet.

"Our friends are very dull, aren't they? What shall we do to make them more interesting?" Frank said loudly, for everyone to hear. "Ladies and gentlemen, I am ordered by Miss Woodhouse to ask what you're all thinking."

"Oh no!" said Emma, laughing. "I don't want that."

"All right then," Frank continued. "Miss Woodhouse

wants you all to say something. It can be one very clever thing, or two quite clever things, or three very dull things, and she promises to laugh at them all."

"That won't be difficult for me," said Miss Bates cheerfully. "I will say lots of dull things as soon as I open my mouth, won't I?"

"Excuse me, Miss Bates," replied Emma quickly. "There may be a problem. You're only allowed to say *three* dull things."

Miss Bates did not understand Emma at first. When she did understand, she blushed and looked hurt.

"Of course. I see what Miss Woodhouse means," said Miss Bates, turning to Mr Knightley. "I will try to keep quiet, and not be so annoying."

"I'm not joining in," said Mrs Elton. "I don't like games like this. They're not right for summer picnics. Pass us, please, Mr Churchill. Pass Mr E, Knightley, Jane and myself. We have nothing clever to say."

"Yes, I have nothing interesting to say to young ladies," agreed her husband. "I'm an old married man now. Shall we walk, my dear?"

"Yes, I'm tired of sitting here so long. Come, Jane," said Mrs Elton. But Jane did not go with them.

"It's interesting to see husbands and wives together," said Frank, watching the Eltons walk off. "They only met a few times in Bath, I hear, before they got **engaged**. I think a man should see a woman in her normal life, with her friends, to understand what she's really like."

Jane, who did not often speak in company, said, "Sometimes men and women get engaged quickly, without really knowing one another. But there's always time for them to think again, before it's too late."

No one said anything for a moment. Then Frank said cheerfully, "Well, I would be useless at choosing a wife. Will you choose one for me, Miss Woodhouse?"

"Shall I find someone like myself?" Emma was enjoying flirting with Frank again.

"Yes, she must have light brown eyes and a lovely nature."

Emma was very pleased. Surely Harriet was perfect for Frank, even if her eyes were blue.

Then Jane stood up. "Shall we join Mrs Elton?" she said to her aunt.

"Yes, of course, my dear," said Miss Bates, and they walked off, followed by Mr Knightley.

After a while, even Emma was tired of Frank's foolish talk. She was very pleased to see the carriages arrive at last to take them all home.

While she was waiting for her carriage, Mr Knightley appeared at her side.

"Emma, how could you be so unkind to Miss Bates?" he said.

Emma blushed and tried to laugh. "How could I help it? It wasn't very bad. I don't suppose she understood me."

"I promise you she did. She has talked about it since. She told me how kind you always are to her, even when her company is so annoying."

"Oh, I know that Miss Bates is a good person, but you know how dull she is!" cried Emma.

"Emma, she is poor. You should feel sorry for her, not laugh at her, in front of others. It was very badly done!"

Emma was too **ashamed** to reply and got into the carriage without speaking. "He is right. I was very unkind to Miss Bates. And I didn't tell him this, or even say goodbye," she thought, and she began to cry.

CHAPTER TEN
Two surprises

The next morning, Emma still felt very ashamed. She decided to visit Miss Bates immediately. Miss Bates was as polite as ever, but did not talk in her usual, cheerful way.

"Jane is going to take a job as a governess," she told Emma, sadly. "Mrs Elton has found her a very superior family, with three little girls. It's only four miles from Maple Grove. At first Jane said no, then suddenly, yesterday evening, she agreed to it. But now she feels very upset and unwell."

Emma felt very sorry for Jane.

When she got back to Hartfield, Mr Knightley and Harriet were there.

"I'm going to London to visit John and Isabella," said Mr Knightley. "I came to say goodbye."

Emma was surprised. "I'm sure he's still angry with me," she thought, sadly.

"Well, Emma, how are my dear old friends?" her father asked. Then he explained to Mr Knightley, "Emma has been to visit Mrs and Miss Bates. She is so kind to them."

Emma blushed. She looked at Mr Knightley and he looked back at her. Then he came towards her and took her hand, but suddenly dropped it. She did not really understand him, but she felt sure that they were friends again. The next moment he was gone.

The following day, news was brought from Richmond which drove all other thoughts away. Mrs Churchill was dead.

"Poor Mrs Churchill. So she *was* very ill," Emma thought. "And poor Mr Churchill. But now Frank will be free and can think about marrying."

One morning, about ten days after Mrs Churchill's death, a message came for Emma, asking her to hurry to Randalls. Emma found Mrs Weston looking very upset.

"What has happened? Something terrible, I know," cried Emma.

"Frank has been here and had some news," Mrs Weston replied. "He came to tell his father that he is engaged . . . " Emma thought of Harriet. " . . . he is engaged to Jane Fairfax! And has been for many months."

Emma jumped with surprise. "Jane Fairfax! You are not serious?"

"Yes, we're all as shocked as you. They've been engaged since October, when they were in Weymouth, and it was kept secret from everybody. I cannot believe it. It has hurt his father and me very much."

Emma began to think of the foolish things she said to Frank about Mr Dixon, about flirting with him in front of Jane, and then about poor Harriet. She felt very ashamed.

"I'm very sorry, Emma. I think it will hurt you even more," Mrs Weston was saying.

"No, you must not be worried about me," replied Emma,

understanding her friend. "I have never been in love with him."

"Oh Emma, that makes me feel much better! Mr Weston and I were very anxious about you – we always hoped that one day you and Frank might marry. And we were sure that you felt the same way."

Emma promised her friend that her heart was not broken and hurried away to think about this shocking news in private.

She was very angry with herself. "Poor Harriet! It's the second time I've done her wrong. She spoke to me about Frank Churchill first, but I still encouraged her. Why didn't I tell her never to think of him?"

Just then she heard Harriet arriving. Her heart jumped.

"Well, Miss Woodhouse!" cried Harriet, coming in. "Isn't it the strangest news you've ever heard – about Jane Fairfax? Mr Weston just told me."

Emma could not understand it. Harriet did not appear to be even a little disappointed.

"Did you have any idea that Mr Churchill was in love with her?" Harriet asked her.

"No, of course not. Didn't I encourage you to hope that he might love you one day?"

"Me! You don't think I care about Mr Churchill?" said Harriet.

"What do you mean?" cried Emma.

"I know we agreed never to say his name, but I was sure you understood me," said Harriet. "He is superior to everyone! How could it be Mr Frank Churchill? The man I was talking about is so much better than him. And you encouraged me to think of him. You said, 'Sometimes surprising matches are made.'"

"Harriet," said Emma slowly. "Are you speaking of Mr Knightley?"

"Of course I am. I told you how he saved me," said Harriet.

"But you were saved by Frank Churchill from the boys," said Emma.

"I was thinking about Mr Knightley at the ball," answered Harriet. "He asked me to dance when Mr Elton refused to. Then I understood how superior he is to all other men."

"Good God!" cried Emma. "What a terrible mistake!"

"But as you say, Miss Woodhouse, sometimes wonderful things do happen."

Emma looked at Harriet in surprise. "Do you think it possible that Mr Knightley loves you?" she asked quietly.

"Yes," said Harriet, "I do."

Emma looked away quickly and said nothing. Why was it so much worse for Harriet to be in love with Mr Knightley than with Frank Churchill? Why was it so painful that Mr Knightley might love Harriet back? She saw the truth at last – Mr Knightley must marry no one but herself.

Later, Emma felt she could not be unhappier. "Today has brought so many horrible surprises," she thought. "I've made so many mistakes. I imagined that I knew everyone's secret feelings, and could plan other people's lives. I was wrong about Frank Churchill, and about Jane Fairfax. I have hurt Harriet. And now I have hurt myself, too."

CHAPTER ELEVEN
Three more weddings

Emma was very upset. First she had to understand herself. "When did I start to love Mr Knightley?" she asked herself. "I cannot remember a time when I did not. But I know that he sees my faults and doesn't love me. How shocked he was when I spoke unkindly to Miss Bates. Maybe he does love Harriet. I've seen them talking together."

By the evening, it seemed that summer was gone. Dark clouds filled the sky, cold rain fell, and the wind shook the leaves from the trees. Emma sat with her father and remembered the sadness they felt on the evening of Mrs Weston's wedding day. "But Mr Knightley came to visit us then," she thought. "If he gets married, Harriet will be the most important person in his life, and it will be my own fault. Oh, why didn't I allow Harriet to marry Robert Martin?"

The next morning, the weather was still wet and grey. But in the afternoon the clouds went away, the sun appeared and it was summer again. Emma hurried outside into the garden for a walk. It was very beautiful after the rain and she began to feel a little better. She was thinking about Mr Knightley in London when, suddenly, she saw him coming towards her.

"I have just got back. Isabella sends her love," he told her. He looked very serious.

"Maybe he told his brother about his plan to marry Harriet, and he didn't like it," Emma thought.

They walked together and Mr Knightley was silent. "Maybe he wants to tell me about his love for Harriet and is afraid to begin," she thought.

She could not bear to be quiet. Trying to smile, she said, "There is some surprising news."

"I've already heard about Jane Fairfax and Frank Churchill," he said, quietly. Then he took her hand in his and held it against his heart. "He has behaved very badly towards you, my dearest Emma."

Emma's heart beat faster. "You're very kind, but I'm not sorry that Frank is engaged. I was never in love with him."

"Really?" said Mr Knightley. "But I could see how much you enjoyed his company."

"I did, but I feel ashamed of the way we **flirted**. Maybe it helped him hide his true feelings for Jane Fairfax."

"Frank Churchill is a lucky man to have found such a wonderful wife," Mr Knightley said, very **seriously**.

Emma was afraid he was thinking about Harriet. Then suddenly he said, "Emma, I must tell you something."

She did not want to hear him say that he loved Harriet. But she knew she had to listen. "Mr Knightley, you can tell me anything, as a friend," she said.

"As a friend . . . that's the problem!" he said. "Oh, dear Emma, can you give me any hope?"

Emma could not speak. She was afraid of waking from the happiest dream.

"Dearest Emma, please give me your answer. If it is no, tell me quickly," said Mr Knightley.

Emma was slowly understanding everything. Harriet was nothing to him, and she was everything.

"I have never loved anyone but you," she said.

Emma was very nearly perfectly happy, but two things troubled her – her father and Harriet. "I can never leave Papa, so I cannot marry while he's alive," she said to herself, and the thought of it made her cry. "And I've done Harriet a great wrong. I'll write to her because I cannot bear to see her, and I'll ask Isabella to invite her to London. Poor Harriet may enjoy visiting London for a while."

The following week, when Harriet was in London, Mrs Weston came to Hartfield with a letter for Emma. It was from Frank and it explained everything.

"He's very sorry for what he has done," she told Emma. "He had to be engaged secretly because of Mrs Churchill, who did not want him to marry."

"But he flirted with me, when he was engaged to Jane," said Emma.

"He was sure you didn't love him and it helped him hide his secret. He thought you guessed that he was in love with Jane, and that he sent her the piano. He nearly told you once, when he first left Highbury."

"How could Jane bear it?" asked Emma.

"She quarrelled with him after Box Hill and broke off their **engagement**," said Mrs Weston. "That's why she agreed to take the governess job which Mrs Elton found."

"I'm afraid I made her unhappy, too," said Emma, blushing to think of how she flirted with Frank at Box Hill. "But I believe she and Frank love each other very much and will be happy together."

———

A few days later, Mr Knightley came to Hartfield with more news.

"I have something to tell you, Emma, and I'm afraid you won't like it," he said. "Harriet Smith is going to marry Robert Martin. I've just heard it from Robert himself."

"I am very surprised, but it doesn't make me unhappy. Tell me everything," cried Emma.

"Robert went to London three days ago on business. I asked him to take some papers to my brother, and John and Isabella invited him to dinner the next day.

He visited the house the day after, too, and was able to speak to Harriet alone."

"I'm truly happy for her," Emma said. "I feel so differently now. I was very foolish before."

"My opinion of Harriet has changed, too," said Mr Knightley. "I've tried to get to know her, because of you, and Robert. So I've talked to her often."

Emma was very happy. "Now I'll be pleased to see Harriet again, and to get to know Robert Martin," she thought.

Mr Knightley spoke again. "My dear Emma, at first, I thought your father might live with us at Donwell. But I've had another idea – that I live at Hartfield."

"I never thought of that," cried Emma happily. "But could you really leave Donwell and live here with my father?"

"I would do anything for you," he said.

———————

Before the end of the year, there were three more weddings. In the autumn, Frank Churchill and Jane Fairfax were married in London, and Harriet Smith and Robert Martin were married in Highbury. A month later, Mr Knightley and Miss Woodhouse stood in the same church in Highbury, as Mr Elton joined their hands in marriage. The wedding was no different to any other wedding, and Mr and Mrs Elton thought that their own wedding had been greatly superior. But the true friends at the wedding saw a perfect match, and two very happy people joined together in marriage.

During-reading questions

Write the answers to these questions in your notebook.

1 Why do Emma and her father feel sad?
2 Why don't Mr Knightley and Mr Woodhouse like Emma's match-making?
3 How does Emma think that she can help Harriet?

1 Why doesn't Emma want Harriet to marry Robert Martin?
2 What don't Mr Knightley and Mrs Weston agree about, and why?
3 Who would Emma like Harriet to marry?

1 How does Harriet reply to Robert Martin's letter?
2 What do Mr Knightley and Emma quarrel about?
3 What does Mr Elton do with the picture of Harriet? What does Emma think this means?

1 Why is Emma annoyed with Mr John Knightley?
2 Who is Frank Churchill and what does Emma think about him?
3 Who does Mr Elton want to marry?

1 Why is Mr Knightley cross with Frank Churchill?
2 What does Emma think about Jane Fairfax?
3 Why does Miss Bates think that Jane is not going to Ireland? And why does Emma think she is not going there?

CHAPTER SIX

1 Who does Frank Churchill want to visit when he leaves Hartfield, and why?
2 What does Emma think of Frank?
3 "There is something between Mr Dixon and Miss Fairfax." What does Emma mean?
4 Why does Frank go to speak to Jane about her hair?

CHAPTER SEVEN

1 What do Emma and Frank talk about while Jane is playing the piano?
2 What does Emma think that Frank wants to say to her when he leaves?
3 Why doesn't Mrs Elton want Jane to get her own letters from the post office? And why does Jane refuse Mrs Elton's help, do you think?
4 Why doesn't Emma like Mrs Elton?

CHAPTER EIGHT

1 Why can Frank come back to Highbury?
2 How does Mr Knightley save Harriet?
3 How does Frank save Harriet?

CHAPTER NINE

1 How does Mrs Elton want to help Jane, and why doesn't Jane want her help?
2 Why does Emma think that Jane goes home early from Donwell?
3 Why is Mr Knightley cross with Emma?

CHAPTER TEN

1 What has Jane decided to do?
2 Where does Mr Knightley go?
3 Why is Emma ashamed when she hears Mrs Weston's news?

CHAPTER ELEVEN

1 Who does Mr Knightley think Emma wanted to marry?
2 Who does Emma think Mr Knightley wanted to marry?
3 Why was Frank Churchill engaged secretly?
4 Why does Mr Knightley want to live at Hartfield?

After-reading questions

1 Look at Chapters Two to Four again. Why did Emma think Mr Elton was in love with Harriet? What did these things really show?
2 Look at Chapters Five to Seven again. What mistakes does Emma make about Jane Fairfax? What really happened?
3 Look at Chapters Seven to Nine again. What mistakes does Emma make about Frank Churchill? What really happened?
4 In Chapter Five why is Mr Knightley cross about Frank Churchill, do you think? What mistakes does Emma make about Mr Knightley in the story?
5 Do you think Emma was wrong to make matches for people? Give reasons for your answer.

Exercises

CHAPTER ONE

1 Write the correct words in your notebook.

1	aruten ....*nature*...........	the way a person usually acts
2	inpinoo	your thoughts about someone or something
3	soxaniu	very worried
4	ruclefeh	happy
5	feerptc	when someone or something is as good as possible
6	persouri	better

CHAPTER TWO

2 Complete these sentences in your notebook, using the names from the box. You can use the names more than once.

Mr Elton	Emma	Mr Woodhouse
Robert Martin	Mr Knightley	Harriet

1 ....*Emma*...... was surprised and worried when she heard that .... was a single man.

2 "Harriet, you cannot compare Mr Martin with ...."

3 Emma thinks that .... wants to please ....

4 .... could see faults in ....

5 " .... will soon feel uncomfortable with her place in society," said ....

6 " .... might never marry because poor .... cannot manage without her."

CHAPTER THREE

3 **Who said this? Who did they say it to? Write the correct names in your notebook.**

1 "Mr Martin has asked me to marry him!"
   Harriet said this to Emma.

2 "You think I should refuse him then?"

3 "I could not visit Mr Martin's wife."

4 "Why do you think her superior to Robert Martin?"

5 "Mr Elton will not marry someone who is below him in society."

6 "Our opinions about men and women are very different."

CHAPTERS FOUR AND FIVE

4 **Write the correct verb form, past simple or present perfect, in your notebook.**

1 "It's strange that Mr Elton **forgot / *has forgotten*** Harriet already."

2 "Frank **wanted / has wanted** to come to Highbury since September."

3 "Frank Churchill **was / has been** in Weymouth a little while ago."

4 "You **decided / have decided** to think badly of Frank Churchill."

5 "Why was **he / has he** been so cross about a young man that he didn't **meet / hasn't met**?"

6 "I **read / have read** Jane's letter twice to Mother already."

7 "We **didn't see / haven't seen** Jane for two years."

8 "I **just met / have just met** Robert Martin in a shop."

CHAPTER SIX

5 **Put these sentences in the correct order in your notebook.**

a .... Jane receives a piano as a present.

b .... Mrs Weston has an idea about Mr Knightley.

c .... Frank visits Mrs and Miss Bates, and Jane Fairfax.

d .... Frank goes to London to get his hair cut.

e ....*1*.... Mr Weston and his son visit Hartfield.

f .... Miss Bates and Jane Fairfax arrive at the party in Mr Knightley's carriage.

g .... Frank and Emma look at the ballroom at The Crown Hotel.

h .... Emma sits by Frank at the Coles's dinner party.

CHAPTER SEVEN

6 **Complete these sentences in your notebook, using the words from the box.**

> dull   silent   quarrel   faults   refused   sigh
> troubled   disappointed   ball   imagined

Emma had no time to ¹ *..quarrel..* with Mr Knightley about the ² .... because Frank suddenly had to go back to Yorkshire. Emma felt very ³ .... that Frank was leaving. Frank seemed ⁴ .... when he said goodbye to Emma. He was ⁵ .... and then she heard him ⁶ .... "Everything feels ⁷ .... without him," she thought when he was gone. But later she thought, "He's a nice young man, but he does have ⁸ .... " When Emma ⁹ .... Frank asking her to marry him, she always ¹⁰ .... him.

CHAPTERS EIGHT AND NINE

7 Complete these sentences in your notebook with *who*, *which* or *that*. Sometimes two answers are possible.

1 Mrs Churchill wanted to come to Richmond, ...*which*... was only nine miles from Highbury.

2 Frank is the only young man in the room .... could be compared to Mr Knightley.

3 Harriet and her friend were stopped by some young boys .... wanted money.

4 Mrs Elton made plans for a large picnic at Box Hill, ... was in a lovely part of the countryside.

5 Mrs Elton, ... was wearing a very large hat, was talking loudly.

6 They came to a place .... looked across the countryside, towards Mill Farm.

CHAPTERS NINE AND TEN

8 Complete these sentences in your notebook using the passive form of the verbs from the box.

save	order	bring	break	drive	keep

1 Mr Woodhouse ......*was*...... safely ....*driven*..... in his carriage.

2 "I .... by Miss Woodhouse to ask what you're all thinking."

3 The following day, news .... from Richmond.

4 Their engagement .... secret from everybody.

5 Emma's heart .... not ....

6 "You .... by Frank Churchill from the boys."

CHAPTER ELEVEN

9 **Are these sentences** *true* **or** *false*? **If the answer is false, write the correct sentence in your notebook.**

1 Emma has never loved Mr Knightley.

false   *Emma has always loved Mr Knightley.*

2 Emma is sorry that Harriet did not marry Mr Elton.

3 Mr Knightley is sure that Emma is in love with him.

4 Emma is ashamed of flirting with Frank Churchill.

5 Emma is very anxious about leaving her father.

6 Mrs Churchill did not want Frank to get married.

7 Mr Dixon sent Jane the piano.

8 Jane broke off her engagement to Frank because she did not love him.

An answer key for all questions and exercises can be found at
www.penguinreaders.co.uk

Project work

1 Choose one of the people in the story and write about them. Use as many of the words from the glossary on pages 78–80, and the words from the box, as you can. Include your own opinion of the person.

> beautiful   clever   handsome   important
> intelligent   kind/unkind   nervous   pretty
> quiet   rich   single   friendly/unfriendly

2 Choose one of these letters to write:
   • Harriet's letter to Robert Martin in Chapter Three
   • Emma's letter to Harriet in Chapter Eleven
   • Frank's letter to Emma in Chapter Eleven

3 What do you think happened in Chapter Nine when Jane and Frank met, as Jane was leaving Donwell and Frank was just arriving? Write their conversation.

4 Compare the book to a film of *Emma*. How are they the same/different? Why did the writer make these changes for the film, do you think?

5 Find out more about life in England or in your own country at the time of Jane Austen.

Glossary

adopt (v.); **adopted** (adj.)
If someone *adopts* another person's child, they become the parent of that child. The child is *adopted*.

annoying (adj.)
If someone or something is *annoying*, they make you feel a little angry.

anxious (adj.)
very worried

ashamed (adj.)
You feel *ashamed* when you feel bad because you have done something wrong.

ball (n.); **ballroom** (n.)
A *ball* is a large party where people dance. The room where the people dance is a *ballroom*.

bear (v.)
to be able to live with something that's difficult

blush (v.)
You *blush* when your face goes pink, for example because you are ashamed or because someone is looking at you.

charming (adj.)
If someone is *charming*, you like them because they say and do nice things.

cheerful (adj.)
happy

circle (n.)
a group of people who know each other and meet often

company (n.)
having other people with you

compare (v.)
to think that someone is (not) as good, kind, etc. as another person

disappointed (adj.)
unhappy because something that you wanted did not happen

dull (adj.)
boring or not interesting

educated/uneducated (adj.)
Someone who is *educated* has been to school and knows a lot. Someone who is *uneducated* has not been to school, or did not go to school for very long.

encourage (v.)
to say someone should do something

engaged (adj.); **engagement** (n.)
When two people get *engaged*, they agree to get married. An *engagement* is when you have agreed to marry someone.

equal (n.)
An *equal* is someone who is the same level as you in *society*, for example they have the same amount of money as you, they are as intelligent as you, etc.

fault (n.)
something that is not good about a person

78

feeling (n.)
You have *feelings* when you are sad, happy or angry, for example. *Feeling* is the noun of feel.

flirt (v.)
to act in a way that shows you like someone

foolish (adj.)
feeling stupid because you have said or done something wrong

gentleman (n.)
a man from a rich family

imagine (v.); **imaginary** (adj.)
You *imagine* something or someone when you have a picture in your head about what they are like. *Imaginary* things are not real.

manage (v.)
to be able to do something and not need help

manners (v.)
Your *manners* are the way that you act when you are with other people. If you have good *manners*, you act in a *polite* way, for example by speaking nicely to someone or opening a door for them.

marriage (n.)
After two people marry, they are in a *marriage*. They have promised to love each other and stay together for all of their lives.

match (n.); **match-making** (n.)
A *match* is when two people are exactly right for each other. *Match-making* is when you try to find a good husband or wife for someone.

natural (adj.)
If you are the *natural* child of someone, your parents were not married when you were born.

nature (n.)
A person's *nature* is the way that they usually act. They can have a happy, kind, or angry *nature*.

opinion (n.)
your thoughts about someone or something

perfect (adj.); **perfectly** (adv.)
You say that someone or something is *perfect* when they are as good as possible. Someone who is *perfectly* happy is very happy.

pleased (adj.); **please** (v.)
When you are *pleased* you are happy. You *please* someone when you make them happy.

polite (adj.); **politely** (adv.)
Someone who is *polite* acts and speaks in a nice way. When you speak *politely*, you do it in a nice way. You have good *manners*.

quarrel (v. and n.)
when two people speak in an angry way because they do not agree

refuse (v.)
to say no to something

sadness (n.)
What you feel when someone you like has gone away. *Sadness* is the noun of *sad*.

serious (adj.) **seriously** (adv.)
Something that is *serious* is important. Someone looks *serious* when they are not smiling. Someone is *serious* when they mean what they say and are not joking. If you say something *seriously* you are not joking.

shocked (adj.)
very surprised, sometimes not in a good way

sigh (v.)
to let air out of your mouth slowly often because you are tired, sad, or in love

society (n.)
Society is all people. Your place in *society* comes from how much money you have, how *educated* you are, what your family is like, etc. People who have more money or went to a better school have a higher place.

superior (adj.)
better

trouble (v.)
to make someone worried or give them problems

upset (v. and adj.)
To *upset* someone is to make them feel unhappy. Someone who is *upset* is not happy because something bad has happened.